Trapped in Space

The Story of Apollo 13

Sophie Alphonso

SCHOLASTIC INC.
New York Toronto London Auckland Sydney
Mexico City New Delhi Hong Kong Buenos Aires

Cover
© VCL/Spencer Rowell/Getty Images

9 1 0   40   12 11

Contents

On April 11, 1970, *Apollo 13* launched from Cape Kennedy Space Center, near Orlando, Florida. The spacecraft was headed for the moon.

Introduction

In 1970, the Apollo program was three years old. Twelve Apollo spacecraft had rocketed into space. On the last two missions, **astronauts** had landed on the moon. Mission 13 was about to begin. In a few days, Commander Jim Lovell and pilot Fred Haise would be walking on the moon—if all went according to plan.

astronauts people who travel in space

Round-Trip to the Moon

Apollo 13 was built to go to the moon and back.

The *Apollo 13* spacecraft was made up of three separate parts: *Odyssey*, the Service **Module**, and *Aquarius*. The original plan was for the astronauts, Jim Lovell, Jack Swigert, and Fred Haise, to fly into space in *Odyssey*, with the Service Module and *Aquarius* attached.

When they got near the moon, Lovell and Haise would board *Aquarius* and fly to the moon. There, they would step out and explore.

Lovell and Haise would then return to *Odyssey. Apollo 13* would return to Earth—but *Aquarius* and the Service Module would be left in space just before the spacecraft entered Earth's **atmosphere**.

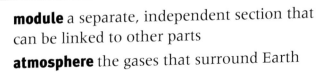

Saturn V

module a separate, independent section that can be linked to other parts

atmosphere the gases that surround Earth

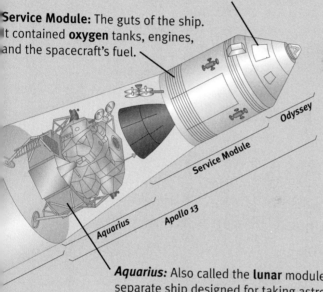

Odyssey: Also called the Command Module. That's where the astronauts lived and worked. Commander Jim Lovell piloted the spacecraft from here, assisted by Jack Swigert.

Service Module: The guts of the ship. It contained **oxygen** tanks, engines, and the spacecraft's fuel.

Odyssey

Service Module

Aquarius

Apollo 13

Aquarius: Also called the **lunar** module. A small, separate ship designed for taking astronauts from *Odyssey* to the moon—and back again. Astronaut Fred Haise was the pilot of this ship.

Saturn V: Launched *Apollo 13*. It was designed to fall off after liftoff.

oxygen a gas found in air. Humans and animals need it to breathe.

lunar having to do with the moon

With three astronauts aboard, Apollo 13 rocketed into space.

1

"We Have Liftoff!"

Commander Jim Lovell was one of the most experienced astronauts in the space program. He had flown nearly seven million miles. There was only one thing left. Lovell wanted to walk on the moon.

On Saturday, April 11, 1970, it looked like Lovell would get his chance. Lovell was strapped into *Odyssey*, the main part of *Apollo 13*. By his side sat *Odyssey* pilot

commander leader

The astronauts walk to the launch pad to prepare for takeoff. Commander Jim Lovell is in the front. *Odyssey* pilot Jack Swigert is behind him. Lunar module pilot Fred Haise is in the rear.

The crew of *Apollo 13* sits in *Odyssey*, getting ready to lift off. The launch is one of the most dangerous parts of a space mission.

Jack Swigert. Next to Swigert was Fred Haise. His job would be to pilot *Aquarius* to a landing on the moon. Jim Lovell would go with him.

A huge roar went up. Flames shot from the engines. The force sent the spacecraft rocketing into the air and pushed the men back against their seats.

"We have liftoff," reported Mission Control in Houston. There, hundreds of scientists and other experts sat glued to their computer screens and dials. For several days, they would watch every detail of the mission. If the spacecraft went 20 feet off course, they would know. If oxygen levels dropped a little low, they would know. If the astronauts' heart rates were a little too high, they would know even that. And hopefully, if something went wrong, they would know how to fix it.

On the ground, Lovell's wife, Marilyn, watched the liftoff. She had a bad feeling in her stomach. Jim's luck had held for three space missions. Could he possibly have enough left for four?

Thousands of miles into space, the crew realizes that something has gone wrong.

2

"We've Had a Problem"

By Sunday morning, Lovell, Haise, and Swigert were out of their space suits. There is no **gravity** in space, so they floated around *Odyssey*, enjoying the ride. Lovell called down to Houston: "We'd like to hear what the news is."

Mission Control reported that the Houston Astros had beaten the Atlanta Braves. There had been an earthquake in

gravity the force that pulls things down toward the surface of Earth and keeps them from floating away into space

At mission control in Houston, Texas, controllers watched the astronauts' TV transmission from space. Fred Haise is on the screen.

the Philippines. Air traffic controllers, whose job was to keep plane traffic moving safely, were still on strike. "But you'll be happy to know the controllers in Mission Control are still on the job," they joked.

On Monday, Mission Control radioed that everything looked perfect. "We're

transmission a broadcast

During the TV transmission, the astronauts clowned around for viewers back on Earth. Here, Jack Swigert looks into the camera.

bored to tears down here."

At 8:24 that night, Lovell filmed his crew for a TV show back on Earth. Haise clowned for the camera. Near the end of the broadcast, he turned a **valve** without warning Lovell. A sudden thump and a hiss made the commander flinch. "Every

valve a movable part that controls the flow of liquid or gas

time he does that our hearts jump in our mouths," Lovell said.

Lovell signed off and shut the camera down. In Houston, Marilyn was watching the show with two of their kids. She smiled, happy to see her husband looking so calm.

Back in *Odyssey*, eight minutes later, Lovell heard another thump. The ship shuddered. Haise is fooling around again, he thought. He looked at Haise to tell him it wasn't funny.

Haise wasn't laughing. He looked scared.

So did Swigert. Strapped in his pilot's seat, he had warning lights flashing red over his head. The ship was losing electrical power fast. "Okay, Houston," Swigert said, "we've had a problem here."

Hundreds of people on Earth scrambled to save three people in space.

3

Lost in Space

Apollo 13 was 200,000 miles from Earth. It was heading toward the moon at several thousand miles per hour. And something had gone very wrong.

In Houston, hundreds of scientists and engineers scrambled to figure out the problem. At 9:22 P.M., Lovell looked out the window and gave them the answer. "We are **venting** something out into

venting releasing

© NASA

When the *Apollo 13* crew reported that they were in trouble, the experts at Mission Control raced to find ways to fix their problems.

space," he radioed. "It's a gas of some sort."

The gas was oxygen. In the Service Module, one of two oxygen tanks had exploded. The other was damaged and losing oxygen fast. The crew's air supply was leaking into space. And that wasn't their only problem.

Deep in the Service Module were three fuel **cells**. The fuel cells mixed oxygen and hydrogen to make water. They also made electricity, which powered almost everything on the ship. Without oxygen, the fuel cells were worthless. Without fuel cells, *Odyssey* was worthless.

From the moment he saw the gas leaking into space, Lovell knew that he would never walk on the moon. His mission now was to get his crew home safe.

In two hours, *Odyssey*'s main supply of oxygen and power would run out. It had back-up batteries and a small oxygen tank. They would last about ten hours. Altogether, *Odyssey* had about 12 hours of power and oxygen left. *Apollo 13* was 100

cells containers

hours from home.

Lovell looked at Haise. "If we're going to get home," he said, "we're going to have to use *Aquarius*."

At the Lovell home in Houston, Marilyn heard about the accident. She turned on the TV. According to ABC, the crew had a 10 percent chance of making it back alive. Marilyn ran to her room, shut the door, and wept.

How do you think Lovell planned to use *Aquarius*?

The astronauts hoped that tiny **Aquarius** *would save their lives.*

The Lifeboat

The men scrambled to get into *Aquarius*. Finally, Lovell yelled up to Swigert, "Shut her down!" It was just before midnight on Monday.

Swigert shut down *Odyssey* and floated through the tunnel into *Aquarius*. He felt terrible. He knew *Odyssey* inside and out. But *Aquarius* was Haise's ship. Swigert could only watch.

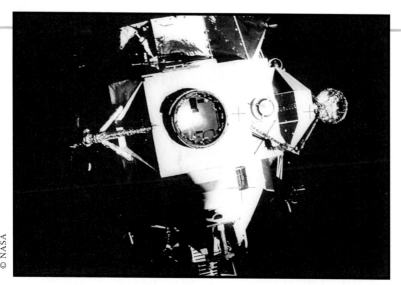

Aquarius was built to take two men from *Odyssey* to the moon. Now it would have to take all three men almost all the way back to Earth.

The men knew they had to be careful. *Aquarius* had its own supplies of oxygen, water, and power. But it was only built to support two men for two days. The trip back to Earth would take four days. And three men had to make it back.

Aquarius also couldn't be used to

re-enter the Earth's atmosphere. The air in the atmosphere is much denser than the air in space. When a spacecraft hits the denser layer, it has to push hard to get through it. The ship gets red hot from the **friction** created by the pushing.

Odyssey had a heat shield to protect it during this part of the trip. *Aquarius* did not. The men would have to use *Aquarius* until they got close to Earth. Then, they would have to climb back into *Odyssey*.

The plan was risky. But it was the astronauts' only hope.

Why couldn't the crew take *Aquarius* all the way back to Earth?

friction the force that slows down objects when they rub against each other

Would there be enough water, oxygen, and power to keep the astronauts alive?

5

Out of Air

Inside *Aquarius,* the astronauts had to be very careful with their supplies. Haise and Mission Control figured the oxygen supply would last. But the astronauts needed to **conserve** water. They had to use most of their water to cool the ship's electrical systems. So each crew member drank just six ounces a day. (A can of soda has 12 ounces.)

conserve to save

To save electricity, they turned off the lights and the computer.

On Tuesday afternoon, *Apollo 13* neared the moon. Haise and Swigert cheered up. The big globe was so close it looked like they could touch it.

In a few hours, the ship would be pulled around by the moon's gravity. They would fire the engines briefly and head for home. They called Lovell over to look at the beautiful view.

Lovell went over and joined them. But his heart wasn't in it. He had dreamed of walking on the moon. Now he just wanted to get home safely.

That wasn't going to be easy. In tiny *Aquarius*, the air was getting dangerous to breathe. There was plenty of oxygen. But

carbon dioxide a gas that's a mixture of carbon and oxygen. People and animals breathe this gas out. Its symbol is CO_2.

every time the men breathed out, they breathed a poisonous gas called **carbon dioxide** into the air.

Normally, a **filter** got rid of this gas. But with three people breathing the air in *Aquarius*, the filters were full. The crew needed to use *Odyssey's* filters.

There was just one problem. *Odyssey's* filters were square. The filters in *Aquarius* were round. The crew had to fit a square peg in a round hole. And they had to do it without the right materials.

Early Wednesday morning, Haise opened a food packet of roast beef. Just then, Mission Control stopped him and asked him to check the CO_2 **gauge**. It read 13. At 15, the filters would no longer work. Soon after, the men would get sick

filter something that cleans liquids or gases as they pass through it

gauge an instrument that measures something

to their stomachs. They would feel faint. Eventually, they would not be able to breathe at all.

Since Monday, Mission Control had been working on the problem. Now, they called up the instructions. The men gathered what they needed from *Odyssey*. And slowly, they put it all together.

Two hours later, they had an odd-looking filter made of cardboard, plastic bags, tape, and socks. They slipped it into place and watched the gauge. In a minute, CO_2 levels began to drop.

Everyone breathed a sigh of relief. "I think I might just finish that roast beef now," Haise said.

The crew is very tired.
Can they keep the spacecraft on course?

6

Drifting Off

By Wednesday night, the crew was cramped, cold, thirsty, and tired. They tried to sleep in *Odyssey*, but all they could do was shiver. With all the systems down, the temperature had dropped to 38 degrees.

They also had another problem. Early Wednesday morning, Mission Control had told Lovell the ship was off course for re-entering the Earth's atmosphere. That

The *Apollo 13* astronauts never landed on the moon. But they got close enough to take this photograph of the moon's surface.

was a huge problem. If the ship didn't hit the Earth's atmosphere at the right angle, it could burn up or bounce off into space.

Now Lovell would have to fire the engines and get the ship back on course.

Normally, astronauts didn't have to steer the spacecraft themselves. Usually,

Apollo 13 astronauts took this photograph of Earth from the spacecraft. The white swirls are storms, and the blue areas are water.

the ship's computer kept track of whether the ship was on course. If it went off course, the computer lined up the ship. Then the computer fired the engines to push the ship back on course.

But now the *Apollo 13* crew couldn't use their computer. So, Lovell had to line the ship by watching Earth or the stars. In addition, he had to use *Aquarius*'s engines to push it back on course. Unlike engines on *Odyssey*, *Aquarius*'s engines were not made to steer the whole ship. It was like steering a heavy wheelbarrow with a long broom handle, Lovell said.

At 10:30 that night, the crew got ready to get the ship back on course. They tried to stay alert. They couldn't afford to make a mistake and waste engine power. They lined up the ship so Earth was visible in its window. Then they fired the engines for 15 seconds.

"Okay, nice work," Mission Control radioed.

Lovell wasn't so sure. "Let's hope it was," he replied.

After eight days in space, planet Earth had never looked so good.

7

Splashdown!

By Thursday evening, Lovell and the others were barely hanging on. Since the explosion, they had hardly slept. Haise was running a high fever.

At one point, Mission Control asked what they could do for the astronauts.

"I'll tell you what we need," Lovell snapped. "We need you to get things right!"

Finally, on Friday morning, Mission

© AP Photo/Wide World Photos

A U.S. Navy aircraft carrier waited for *Odyssey* to splash down in the Pacific Ocean. Then a helicopter from the carrier rushed to the scene.

Control radioed up. "Hang in there. It won't be long now."

Not long after, Swigert went up into *Odyssey*. First, he had to release the Service Module. As it floated away, the astronauts looked on in shock. An entire side of it had been ripped off when the oxygen tank exploded.

A Navy diver was lowered from the helicopter to *Odyssey*. He helped each astronaut one by one into a cage that lifted them to the helicopter.

Finally, around 10:30, they powered up *Odyssey*. Lovell and Haise climbed back in. Next, they let *Aquarius* go. "Farewell *Aquarius*, and we thank you," said Mission Control.

The astronauts strapped themselves into *Odyssey*. They had one final worry on their minds. Had the explosion cracked

The helicopter took the astronauts to the Navy aircraft carrier. From left to right: Astronauts Fred Haise, Jim Lovell, and Jack Swigert.

the heat shield on *Odyssey*? If so, they would burn alive when they entered Earth's atmosphere.

"Gentlemen," Lovell said. "I suggest you get ready for a ride."

Odyssey dropped toward Earth, gaining speed on the way. The men thanked Mission Control for getting them this far.

Then, as *Odyssey* hit the Earth's atmosphere, the crew's radio died. If everything went okay, they would have contact again in three minutes.

People across the country were glued to their TVs. In the Lovell house, Marilyn and her children watched in silence.

One minute passed. Then two. Then three. Mission Control heard nothing. Four minutes passed. Still nothing.

Almost five minutes later, Swigert's voice came through. "Okay!" he said.

The astronauts were alive! At Mission Control everyone cheered. Marilyn Lovell hugged her son so hard he cried out.

The ship splashed down in the Pacific Ocean. Lovell pumped his fist into the air.

"Fellows," he said. "We're home."

Spaced Out

The *Apollo 13* crew had hoped to walk on the Moon. But they were happy just to walk on Earth again.

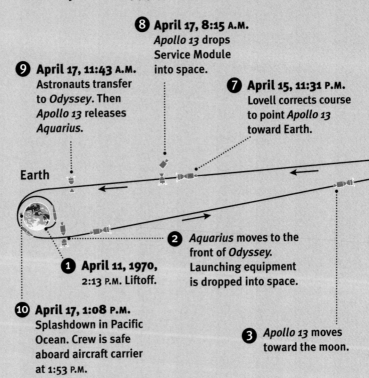

8 April 17, 8:15 A.M.
Apollo 13 drops
Service Module
into space.

9 April 17, 11:43 A.M.
Astronauts transfer
to *Odyssey*. Then
Apollo 13 releases
Aquarius.

7 April 15, 11:31 P.M.
Lovell corrects course
to point *Apollo 13*
toward Earth.

Earth

1 April 11, 1970,
2:13 P.M. Liftoff.

2 *Aquarius* moves to the
front of *Odyssey*.
Launching equipment
is dropped into space.

10 April 17, 1:08 P.M.
Splashdown in Pacific
Ocean. Crew is safe
aboard aircraft carrier
at 1:53 P.M.

3 *Apollo 13* moves
toward the moon.

Ron Carboni © Scholastic Inc.

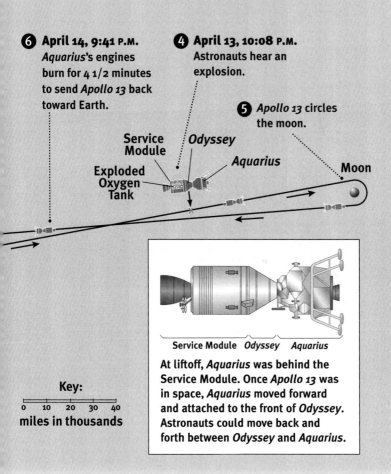

6 April 14, 9:41 P.M.
Aquarius's engines burn for 4 1/2 minutes to send *Apollo 13* back toward Earth.

4 April 13, 10:08 P.M.
Astronauts hear an explosion.

5 *Apollo 13* circles the moon.

Service Module

Odyssey

Aquarius

Exploded Oxygen Tank

Moon

Key:

0   10   20   30   40
miles in thousands

Service Module *Odyssey* *Aquarius*

At liftoff, *Aquarius* was behind the Service Module. Once *Apollo 13* was in space, *Aquarius* moved forward and attached to the front of *Odyssey*. Astronauts could move back and forth between *Odyssey* and *Aquarius*.

Glossary

astronauts *(noun)* people who travel in space

atmosphere *(noun)* the mixture of gases that surrounds Earth

carbon dioxide *(noun)* a gas that's a mixture of carbon and oxygen. People and animals breathe this gas out. Its symbol is CO_2.

cells *(noun)* containers

commander *(noun)* leader

conserve *(verb)* to save

filter *(noun)* something that cleans liquids or gases as they pass through it

friction *(noun)* the force that slows down

objects when they rub against each other

gauge *(noun)* an instrument that measures something

gravity *(noun)* the force that pulls things down toward the surface of Earth and keeps them from floating away into space

lunar *(adjective)* having to do with the moon

module *(noun)* a separate, independent section that can be linked to other parts

oxygen *(noun)* a gas found in air. Humans and animals need it to breathe.

transmission *(noun)* a broadcast

valve *(noun)* a movable part that controls the flow of liquid or gas

venting *(verb)* releasing